The Monday Morning Feeling

A book of comfort for sufferers

Joep P.M. Schrijvers

With drawings by
Peter van Straaten

CYAN

First published in Dutch as *Het maandagmorgengevoel: Een troostboek voor wekenden* by Scriptum Publishers, Schiedam, 2004
(Translator: Jonathan Ellis)

This translation first published in 2005 by:

Marshall Cavendish Business
An imprint of Marshall Cavendish International (Asia) Private Limited
A member of Times Publishing Limited
Times Centre, 1 New Industrial Road
Singapore 536196
T: +65 6213 9300
F: +65 6285 4871
E: te@sg.marshallcavendish.com
Online bookstore: www.marshallcavendish.com/genref

and

Cyan Communications Limited
119 Wardour Street
London W1F 0UW
United Kingdom
T: +44 (0)20 7565 6120
E: sales@cyanbooks.com
www.cyanbooks.com

A CIP record for this book is available from the British Library

ISBN 981 261 811 2 (Asia & ANZ)
ISBN 1-904879-40-3 (Rest of world)

Printed and bound in Singapore

THE MONDAY MORNING FEELING

Good morning

This life is a hospital where every patient is consumed with a desire to change beds. One may prefer to lay and suffer near the stove, while the other thinks that he will recover by the window.

Charles Baudelaire, *Le spleen de Paris*

Finally, in the third place, and that seems the most important, it is impossible to overlook how much culture is based on the renunciation of passion, how much it is precisely the repression of powerful passions that is its basic premise.

Sigmund Freud, *Civilisation and its Discontents*

Morning, gorgeous

CONTENTS

PREFACE

It's something we know all too well: that nagging feeling in the stomach, legs that seem unable to carry any weight, arms that are drained of strength. There is no better indicator of the terror that awaits us than our own body with its tinted observations. Just look outside: the brown of the houses turns to gray and the green drains from the trees. An oppressive cloud causes us to catch our breath. Once again the moment is upon us. A shock reverberates through our systems at the realization of those ponderous day-to-day cares. Any memory of friendly recreation, of pleasant company, of gentle frivolity evaporates. The poets moan and sigh:

> Monday morning in the rain
> Cannot face it yet again
> Cold and forlorn faces
> Pass us as we wait,
> Cars by the thousand
> In search of a jam
> But one thing is certain
> We'll all arrive late.[1]

The weekly transformation and disguise is complete. We can once again become employee and colleague. It is Monday. Monday morning.

Welcome, dear Reader, to this depressive essay about yourself and about me: an old-fashioned grumpy story that is certainly critical and undoubtedly somber, but which may not completely end on a minor note.

It is worth remembering that this is an essay. Where the scientist proves and tests, where the philosopher argues and rejects, where the lawyer judges and sentences, there the essayist suggests and imagines. The essayist is somebody who roams the no man's land between fiction and non-fiction in the hope of gaining a glimpse of a reality that may otherwise pass unnoticed. For this the essayist wields style weapons that must remain forbidden for "normal" books: magnification, exaggeration, humiliation, provocation, far-fetched imagery, and metaphors. The essayist goes to work like a cartoonist.

And yet I adhere to a traditional form.[2] In the first chapter we will take a closer look at the perils of Monday morning. En passant, I will discuss the importance of those unpleasant movements in the midriff. The portrait gallery of colleagues and superiors that follows will, thanks to the recognition it will certainly trigger, prepare us for stronger medicine against the Monday morning feeling. But before we can actually take this medicine, we must first pass through the fire of the "prophets of prosperity" and other charlatans who, with their glib tongues, wander the corridors of business schools and universities. After that, we cast ourselves off into our life of rage. We shall, no we *must* acknowledge that the "Monday morning feeling" is an inevitable companion throughout the life of any professional. The only medicine that brings any relief is acceptance and comfort, virtues that are rarely met in the fast and furious world of business babes and other career makers.

If, as you read this essay, you suddenly think: "I do not recognize this; things aren't as bad as this," then understand that this book provides an antidote for those moments when the unpleasant aspects of your life attack you or finally force themselves onto you. For nothing comforts and revives better than the awareness that things can be a lot worse. That is the knowledge that this book offers.

So let's really get grumpy. Put the songs of Leonard Cohen on your record player; keep the bottle cold, and the Prozac at hand. We are about to enter the gloom ...

Part I

The Monday morning feeling

Why don't you just stay at home on
Mondays?

1 In the bedroom

First we'll take you over live to an average bedroom, some-where, say, in Milton Keynes (England). It is 06.43 on Monday morning. The house—and the family in it (husband, wife, and 1.8 children)—is in turmoil. Next to me is James. He is an accountant at a financial brokerage. Last week, he attended the workshop "Dress for success." What will James be wearing today?

- Good morning, James.
- And good morning to you.

- What will you be wearing today?
- Well—the usual...

- And that is...?
- Look. I can choose...

- I see. Choose! Why don't you tell our viewers exactly what you have got in your wardrobe?
- I've got three dark gray suits.
  I'm aiming at 14 eventually.
  Suitable suits advised by ...
  Selected by ...

The only real partner of professionals, the man that really understand us:

CECIL GEE

With the French pronunciation, Cécil Jzay

The only real tailor in England.

Genuine Italian suits.

Made in Milan by an Italian tailor.

I have 14 shirts.

Eight white, four with a stripe, two blue with white collars.

18 ties.

Four belts.

Eight pairs of shoes.

20 pairs of socks—knee length

And none with Mickey Mouse on them.

14 boxer shorts.

- So what will you be wearing today, James?
- Today it'll simply have to be this dark gray suit. I have an extremely important meeting with this incredible account.

- Never bothered by that Monday morning feeling?
- Sorry—my mobile.
  Yes? Hello. Hello?
  Yes, no
  Yes
  Yes.
  What? No. Never.

- Thanks for the interview.
- Yes, tell me it's not true.
  BLOCKHEAD

Is it really like that? Probably. There are always blockheads who are immune to the Monday morning feeling.

They are so delighted to be able to put on their work costume that they completely lose sight of any dignity and freedom. They miss out on those weekly recurring emotions—sufferings as these emotions used to be called in the past—that are part of working life.

2 Sufferings

The Monday morning feeling is unmistakably an emotion. It visits us, begins, emerges quickly or slowly, persists, and disappears—or not. I prefer to speak of sufferings because this medieval term expresses the true essence of mental moods far better than the term "emotion" that, in the experience economy and in management training, has been stripped of its claws. We do not, after all, choose emotions; we undergo them. They are more often the cause of discomfort than of pleasure.

The Monday morning feeling is a complexity of feelings. Do we not, in those short hours at the start of the week, sometimes experience sorrow, and at other times disgust and anxiety? Does the Monday morning feeling therefore have a number of guises depending on which emotion is the most dominant? Let us briefly review the various components. What sufferings lie at the basis of our Monday morning feeling?

"No, he's just. . . throwing up I think"

Distaste

Every theory about human behavior should begin with a disser-
tation on vomiting. It is not the mind that is the measure of
right and wrong but the midriff. That is where decisions about
quality, about what is good and correct, are made. Nausea is
nothing more than a natural reaction to something our body
judges undesirable. Whenever food or drink is placed before us
with an unappetizing aroma or a rancid taste, we refuse to eat
or drink it. And if, by accident, it still worms its way inside, our
body hastens to eliminate it through any opening it can find.
The next time that something similar is placed before us, our
body—as the perfect judge it is—lets us know immediately that
such concoctions are highly unwelcome. We turn up our nose,
we refuse, and we feel contractions in our stomach: we are
going to throw up—we feel disgusted.

Many people feel queasy on a Monday morning and retch
despairingly through the morning. And rightly so. The feeling
that prevents threats and disasters in our body is the same one
that is active in our daily lives, at home, on the street, in politics, and in our jobs. We also use these uncontrolled contractions in our midriff in our vocabulary: what a nauseating man,
that left a bad taste in my mouth. We make use of all sorts of
expressions that have been transplanted from their purely
bodily context into the social and organizational context. The
question is: what is so distasteful about Monday morning?
What causes such discomfort with work?

Fear

Quite a few people are bothered by fear. They find it difficult to get to sleep on Sunday evening or wrestle themselves awake in the early hours of the morning, plagued by a quick succession of strange and threatening images of "the Company."

No sooner has one bossy secretary disappeared before another, laden with chains, makes his or her dismal entrance and a spotty, pock-marked client shouts in our face, his or her nose getting longer while his or her ears assume satanic proportions. Do we not see ourselves being called in by the project manager to explain why the budget has been exceeded or why our goals have not been met? Do we not hear, in that world of dreamy slumber, the sarcastic tone, the dressing down, and see his or her index finger pointing to the door? Fear has many faces but only one intention: to warn us of danger. Our body reacts with perspiration, with fidgeting arms and legs, and with watchfulness.

That is why we sleep so badly: our bodies, that have taken control of us, are permanently on alert. It is code orange, code red, it tells us, and it doesn't permit us to keep guard like sleeping marines. And the body, which has been lulled to rest during the weekend, takes the real and imagined threats of work and throws them into sharp contrast during Sunday night, just as we are better able to spot a yacht on a calm sea and in good weather rather than during a storm and torrential rain. That is why so many sleep so badly when the week is about to begin.

Rage

We are all familiar with it: the feeling that, as you sit on a hot day bumper-to-bumper in yet another tailback, suddenly takes control of you and makes you want to lash out and kick aside all those cars near you and makes you desperately wish you had fitted caterpillar tracks under your Fiat Panda that would allow you to flatten all the obstacles put in your way. Now when we become aware of that feeling in our bodies, we talk about rage or anger, or, in its milder variant, irritation. From time immemorial, this emotion has rightly been associated with a desire to remove or destroy everything that blocks our path. It is a healing passion, because, like all emotions, it helps us survive. It is hardly surprising that many Monday morning sufferers are buried under the debris of fury and anger: "Sod it—do I really have to go to that bloody job? And if that bitch starts whingeing, then I'll bite off her ugly head and take the biggest hacksaw I can find and set about that disgusting body ..." We all have our own rages, big or small. Doesn't this emotion lay at the root of the Monday morning feeling that rules us and can best be summed up in the words: "Oh piss off ..."?

Sorrow

We now come to the last ingredient of the Monday morning feeling: sorrow. You may say to me: "Isn't sorrow, that emotion, rather exaggerated, just a bit over the top to describe the Monday morning feeling?" No, I would answer, absolutely not. In fact, the other three feelings—distaste, fear, and rage—could, if necessary, be excluded from the mixture that makes up the Monday morning feeling, but sorrow could on no account be dropped. It is always there, just like tealeaves in the tea. On the other hand, I don't wish to pretend that every Monday morning herds of employees weep over their cornflakes, because that weekly recurring collective symphony of sobs is about to begin. Tears are just an outer expression. The sorrow of Monday morning is quieter, and therefore all the more harrowing.

Sorrow is essential during those first few hours of the working week, and the reason is simple. Our body, our faithful compass, tells us that we will soon lose something or that we have already lost it. Something that is part of us—something that is trusted, voluntary, and pleasant—removes itself and our bodies react with contractions of the stomach, inactivity, depression, and a desire for seclusion. It tells us that we will only regain our health and strength when we have enjoyed the rest that is essential if we are to overcome the feeling of loss that has surfaced. That is why, on Monday morning, so many people are reserved, work (if they actually do any work) by themselves, and indicate that they do not wish to be disturbed—and you know why: they are mourning and trying to recover from the loss. Everybody who knows the Monday morning feeling is aware of this sorrow, even if many call it by different names: "I've no energy, I'm a little down, I'm not in the mood," is what they say.

Every Monday morning, we lose something; actually, we lose something every time we hoist ourselves into our professional straitjacket. What that loss is, is something I shall return to later. For now, it suffices to say that sorrow is an essential ingredient in this mishmash of feelings.

Pervasive malaise

And so we see that people who suffer from the Monday morning feeling are afflicted with distaste, fear, rage, and sorrow. Often in varying proportions. For one, distaste comes to the fore, another lays paralyzed by fear waiting for the alarm clock to go off, and yet another feels defiance and resistance coursing through his or her veins—but the feeding ground for all of them is despondency.

We could argue that the Monday morning feeling is a recurring feeling. But it is not as simple as that. We shall see that the Monday morning feeling is nothing more than a pervasive malaise which goes hand in hand with professionalism. A malaise that is currently more powerful than ever. Before we deal with this, however, it will be helpful to take a closer look at the guises in which the Monday morning feeling appears.

3 Faces of malaise

At the office we meet various Monday morning types. Each of these has his or her own characteristic behavior and, in the mix of emotions, one that stands out above the rest. With a little practice, you will easily be able to recognize them in your department or business unit. We will start with an easy one: the drunk.

And, may I ask, what exactly is wrong
with the way I sit here every morning?

Drunk

This type is rather shabby on the outside and nonchalant on the inside. He jovially enters the department with a feigned firm step. He greets everybody as if he is visiting his local after a long absence: "Hey, Fred. Morning Trudy, my little darling." His skin is loose except around his stomach. That's where the tension is. The tail of his shirt hangs out of his trousers, his tie knot is halfway down his shirt, and on the shoulders of his jacket we see—even at this early hour—a dusting of white flakes. He has hastily plastered back his hair with some gel.

If we consider the mix of emotions that the drunk has on a Monday morning, then recklessness is the one that springs out. He is no longer alert to the potential dangers that may lay in wait for him. He has numbed both his anxieties and sorrows with the substances he enjoys so much. We can smell the fear on the lips of the drunk.

Battleaxe

She comes in, goes straight to her desk, and puts down her bag with a loud crash as if to say, "I'm here, because I have to be and don't you dare get in my way." She turns the key angrily in the lock on her filing cabinet (she is the only one who ever bothers to lock it) and, with a growl, removes a number of documents. She then stamps off to the coffee corner in the corridor, looking angrily at everybody around her. Nobody talks to her and she talks to nobody. Everybody is wary of the eruption. Are they dancing here on the edge of a volcano? The battleaxe has laid down her boundaries; anybody who trespasses can expect trouble.

We are dealing here with a wrathful type who is prepared to blow up and destroy any obstacle that obstructs him or her. For the battleaxe, the world is littered with rocks, hunks of meat, and other obstacles.

ADHD

Every company has them and everybody knows them: those industrious men and women who have already done their week's work before the week has even started. They set off to the office before the sun has risen. Six o'clock, seven o'clock—the unbridled and intemperate are already at their post. And when the dejected have finally dragged themselves into the office building, the others have already answered and forwarded all their emails and have updated and distributed the project planning. If luck's against you, then they'll *just* give you a call on your mobile while you're in the tailback feeling like nothing on earth because the week's just started. They even begrudge you your Monday morning feeling. "It's me. I *just* wanted to phone because there are a few appointments this week and I *just* thought I check with you. Can you make it?" You sigh and give a short reply, because you want to be rid of the caller and promise yourself for the umpteenth time that in future you'll *just* ignore him or her. These are, by the way, the same shameless types who *just* ring you late in the evening just to ask you one little question or even dare to ring you when you have a day off.

ADHD types suffer the most—in addition to sorrow—from fear. They don't run away, nor, as so often happens, do they become passionately immobilized by the Monday morning feeling, but find refuge instead by advancing and attacking.

Good weather

She is voluptuous, friendly, and warm. And when she comes in, she really comes in. The Battleaxe may growl, the home queen is all attention and she is so present that it is impossible to avoid her. She laughs, chats, and asks with complete sincerity, while you are deeply immersed in mourning because Monday morning is but a few hours old, how you enjoyed your weekend. "My god," you think, "what a question. It was, of course, wonderful but do you, with that fake happy smile, have to rub salt into the wound? Just as I am desperately trying to forget how enjoyable and delicious the weekend was and trying to use every ounce of my determination to get my tortured mind onto a narrow track, you have to go and ask me with that artificial friendliness and joviality: how was your weekend? Piss off," you think and then get annoyed at yourself because you only think it and don't dare to say it out loud, because she really does mean things for the best, and so you think: "Just piss off, you bitch!"

It is rather difficult to fathom the emotional make-up of the home queen. I personally think it is all because she has suffered an enormous sadness. She is an example of good-weather players, the happy sisters and those hearty friends, who, when they are alone and think they are unobserved, immediately set aside their amiable mask and immediately expose their depressing and somber nakedness.

Off sick

Every Monday morning, the world of commerce is the victim of a weekly recurring epidemic. Hundreds of thousands of people suffer from it, all meters are off the dial, the bells ring, and the sirens scream: people groan, people wail, people suffer. At countless places, HR is at the ready and listens to colleagues: "I can't come in." "I simply can't manage it." And if they then ask what is the matter, then they hear a whole list of complaints: stomach ache, nausea, and vicious stabs of pain in the lower back. There is a lot of suffering on the first day of the working week. A remarkable fact is that the complaints increase when the weather is fine and sunny and when it is nasty and raining. The Monday morning epidemic also hits people hard on mornings after a Sunday evening football match.

What emotional palette does this suggest to us? People have such an aversion to having to go to their work that it is hardly surprising that their limbs refuse to function—it is disgust.

I suppose everybody else is sick again?

4 The start of the misery

There you are then, in your own little cell with its little half steamed-up window that looks out onto a tiny lawn where the mud is clearly showing through the grass and the wild rose bushes that form a hedge are rambling out of control. Wherever you look in the street, you see squares with the same dusty, straggling gray–green bushes. The sky is clear. Everything is so near, yet so far. You look down at your hands that move like foreign creatures across the keyboard. Are they yours? Are those the hands that have caressed so passionately? The veins are blue and swollen. There is a horizontal dash on the "f" and the "j". Are those meant for touch typists, so that they can orientate themselves by feel alone? Mindlessly you once again stare outside. Two boys are poking a stick into something that must be the corpse of a bird. A scientific education cannot start too soon, you think. You sigh and once again type in a few codes. Let's check the emails.

It is not clear when the Monday morning feeling actually begins. The apparently specific time indication could set us off on a wild goose chase. Some people adhere strictly to the definition: the Monday morning feeling starts in the early hours of Monday—let's say around six o'clock. Others, who prefer a

Do you want to check your post,
or should we wait a bit?

wider definition, maintain that the feeling already begins on Friday evening, when everybody rushes home at a speed that is considerably higher than that on other days of the week.

Personally, I believe that the Monday morning feeling actually starts earlier than its name suggests. For many people, it begins on Sunday evening, when people drag themselves up the stairs of their houses into a claustrophobic little room on the first floor, full of cupboards, the ironing board, a white Ikea desk, and a computer (naturally with an ADSL connection and wifi 802.11g), to log into the server of "the Company," which naturally fails because it's too busy. This could be the epitome of the knowledge economy: doing your work everywhere and nowhere with modern equipment—in the evening, on a Sunday, in the last hours of the night. As the economy becomes increasingly flexible, so the borders of discomfort shift until there are no longer any borders and everything has become economy.

5 Stages in the Monday morning feeling

The Monday morning feeling has, in common with all processes, clear stages; we can distinguish the following four:

1. final blooming
2. pleasant nostalgia
3. debilitating distaste
4. inevitable stupefaction.

It is useful to know these stages. Not so that we can intervene (that won't succeed), but so that we can assess what is happening to us now and will happen to us in the future. In earlier times, people would say that if you knew what suffering was going to overtake you, the pain would not be so severe. Unexpected suffering is always more intense.

It's strange, you know, when you
think it's actually Monday

Final blooming

The first stage is that of *final blooming*. It is the stage in which the senses are extra stimulated. We see colors more sharply, hear sounds more intensely, and everything that is set in front of us tastes better. It is as if the body does its job one final time at full power. It knows that a period is imminent in which life will not be ruled by pleasant sensations, but by unpleasant ones. One last meal, one last desire.

Which of us does not recognize this stage? It is the rose that blooms in all its glory before withering and dying. It is the final recapitulation of the theme in a symphony before the timpani brings an end to it. It is the young professional who, by now 25 or 30, prolongs his or her adolescence with travel and parties. We linger a while in bed, feel the crisp sheets, the softness of the sounds, the intimacy of the one lying next to us. That is typical for this stage in the Monday morning feeling: we experience just for a moment, just one last time the pleasant things of life. We are for a while a free person, a *homo ludens*. We turn over just one more time.

Get up? In this weather?

Pleasant nostalgia

And then we slip into the next stage, that of *pleasant nostalgia*. A characteristic of this stage is the broad palette of feelings that occur. A pleasant feeling is mixed with a sorrowful, sad feeling. This mix is very seductive, largely because of the presence of the pleasant feeling. We know this mixture as *nostalgia*. The memories of a happy time are tempered by the sadness that that time is now past:

Schön ist die Jugendzeit, die kommt nicht mehr.

We conjure it up with holiday snaps, by reminiscing about the good old days in social situations.

The Monday morning feeling carries this nostalgia in its womb. We are reminded of the freedom of the weekend and of the joys of summer and, at the same time, we know that these are gone. We grow quiet and daydream, for we know that there is a living to be earned. After all, we were banished from Paradise.

Today I'm doing everything by fax

Debilitating distaste

The third stage, *debilitating distaste,* does not creep up on us like a pleasant nostalgia following the final blooming, but generally announces itself with shock and awe tactics. In this stage, many experience distaste, sometimes even disgust. The images of "the Company" become more vivid. We see that underhanded colleague loom up before us, and that untrustworthy boss, that nagging customer, that whingeing employee. We begin to retch slightly. The body is reacting perfectly, we think. Because as I mentioned earlier, our body is disgusted by things that are bad for us. That's the way it works. Even for the company where we return on Monday. We instinctively back away because our body knows it is damaging for us.

In some people, this stage is ruled by fear. They anticipate all sorts of threats—both real and imagined—that are laying in wait for them during the coming week. A paralysis takes hold of them.

Inevitable stupefaction

And finally we reach the fourth stage: *inevitable stupefaction*. We take a deep breath and swallow hard. We give up any last shred of resistance and try—unsuccessfully—to rid ourselves of any sorrow, because we are fully aware that such feelings make no difference and that we can better go about our work with a smile on our face than with a frown. Because if we allow ourselves to remain in that Monday morning feeling, we simply double our burden: we *have* to do our work *and* we're in a rotten mood. This is one of the first things that anybody learns in his or her career: close your eyes, jump, and pretend that you're having fun. We later learn that it is impossible to avoid discomfort in our work.

Many people have discovered that if, during this stage, you resort to ritual behavior, you very quickly—thank God!—achieve an adequate structure in your awareness (focus is what management gurus always call this). You may use anything you like for this. It starts by putting on your work clothes so that you transform yourself into an official, quickly dumping the children at school, and racing off to the first meeting with your project team. Next, you deal with all those piled up messages, fish around for the latest snippet of gossip, and swallow your first Alka-Seltzer. And with that, you have completed the transformation to colleague.

6 Opinions about Monday morning sufferers

If we were to hold a survey among family and friends, and colleagues and bosses, then we would get a limited number of popular opinions about the Monday morning feeling. I have isolated three separate opinions. We will give each of these its own color, thus bowing to the popular feeling among the public that any categorization only has value if it has a color attached to it. Whether we are dealing with change models, styles of thinking, or terrorist threats, we have to give it a color. And so we must do the same with Monday morning sufferers.

Color Judgement	Red	White	Blue
MM sufferer suffers from:	Lack of moral fiber	Spreadsheet disease	Vapors
And is thus a:	Weakling	Victim	Faker
Who says:	Can't	Won't	Wouldn't dare
And sacrifices:	Duty	Self-respect	Performance

For each of these, I will deal with the factors that are responsible for it, which slogan—either implicitly or explicitly—is chanted, and which core value is threatened.

Lack of moral fiber (red)

You are out of luck if, as Monday morning sufferer, you find yourself landed with a red boss and red colleagues. Time and again you will feel it resounding through your very innards: "weakling, wimp." This is nothing more than the echo of what they really feel about you, that you lack character, you're a limp dick, a plonker, a fairy. They will show you no sympathy when you stumble into the office with a wimpy Prozac grin on your face. They are already there, powerful, energetic, while you drag yourself desperately towards your office chair and the coffee machine. At each step, that one little voice gets louder and louder until it thunders out the echo of what your boss and colleagues really think about you: wanker, wanker. And that's exactly what you are: an employee who doesn't feel like doing anything and can't even make yourself feel like it.

It's pretty awful for you if you have so little willpower and your bosses show you no consideration. You try to grit your teeth but it is as if your mouth is full of marshmallow that prevents you doing it. You want to, but you can't.

And do you hear the slogans that these red types throw around: "Accept your responsibility, accept your responsibility."

If only it were that easy. You know exactly what you have to do and where your duties lie. That isn't the problem. You simply can't do it ... as if your will has on this Monday morning taken a day off. And it isn't exactly nice that your nose is constantly being rubbed in the basic value of your department and your company—duty. Anybody who works has to fulfill his or her duties, precisely, accurately ... and without objection. For anybody who chases after virtue without pleasure, is not at all virtuous. Red is the color of threat, heat, and hell. Red is the color of those who conclude that your Monday morning feeling means you are an immoral person.

Resistance to spreadsheet disease (white)

Leave home one rainy, autumn Monday morning not too early, so that the chance is good that you find yourself in a major tailback. Then look around you: that one there—the one moving her lips—is already holding her fifth meeting on her mobile; and that one there—the one with the fat bald head and a pale face—is drinking water from a baby's bottle; and that one there is clenching her teeth and gripping the steering-wheel so hard that her knuckles are turning white. Three cars, 300,000 cars, 3 million cars, all creeping along towards those glass, air-conditioned cells with their ergonomic chairs, desks, and screens. Here one thing rules supreme: the spreadsheet.

MBA-ers

The offices where once stout capitalists, with fat cigars clenched between their teeth, ruled with an iron fist are now dominated by trained, hygienically manufactured MBA-ers, who love telling you about the marathons they regularly run. They talk about t-factors, billability, added value, and some even dare to speak aloud the s-word: shareholder value. Their world has become one enormous spreadsheet, a hybrid concoction of human and spreadsheet cells. They are interested in but one thing: money. Customers, employees, citizens, pets, and land-scapes—all must step aside for that one figure at the bottom of the spreadsheet that indicates the profit of "the Company." That is their world.

Do you really think it strange that currently so many people barely tolerate Monday mornings? Wouldn't you also suffer if you were reduced to a spreadsheet cell? No, the aversion to Monday morning is a potent instrument with which to measure the quality of our organizations. This feeling is a hallmark: it shows *what* a company is and *how* it operates. But let us not allow ourselves the illusion that it would be possible to design an organization that does not evoke the Monday morning feeling. The malaise is always there, wherever you look. It is simply made worse than it need be by the sickness called "spreadsheet disease."

People who judge the Monday morning feeling in this way say that any depression is a veiled protest against our economic order that isn't about anything anymore, not about customers, not about professionalism, not about employees. The core value from which they set out cannot be better described than with the word "respect." That is what is so desperately lacking in our companies: respect for each other and for the beautiful things that we make.

I have reserved the color white for people who think of things in this way. A color that signifies purity, virginity, and virtue.

Vapors (blue)

"Don't make such a fuss." I regularly hear mothers and fathers say this to their children. Good, I think, give them another future neurosis. Just carry on like that and breed the necessary victims for trainers and coaches. This youthful drama, this pathology, repeats itself every Monday morning in countless companies. Here again you hear them thinking and whispering: "Don't make such a fuss." The judgment passed by blue people on those suffering from the Monday morning feeling is far from tender. They think of them as hypocrites, as bunkers-off. With a bit of bad luck, they are soon known as fusspots.

I once knew a manager who, if one of his subordinates suffered from the tiniest thing, immediately went into overdrive. It's no longer allowed, I know, but he would have liked nothing better than to have grabbed a whip and, like a true slave driver, beaten the docility and sloth out of that unfortunate subordinate. That is the most profound judgment passed on you by blue types: that you are a fusspot and that you are, with your Monday morning feeling, nothing more than a moaner, a poser who acts out your suffering in the most appalling way and who is unjustly lamenting because, quite honestly, you could just as easily get on with things and do your job like a man and help raise the turnover, and that he, your boss, is fully aware of what you are doing: work, you bugger, work!

The deepest value to which such a slave driver aspires is performance. You've been employed to perform and for nothing else. The rest you can leave at home. Such a boss attributes your Monday morning feeling to a laziness that he or she views

Well, OK, if you're really feeling that bad,
perhaps you should go home after all

as the defining aspect of your character. Don't fuss is his or her motto.

I would like to offer you here some comfort if you suffer such injustice, because, as we shall see later, the shirker is the greatest hero in the farce that we know as work. You are on the side of the good guys.

I have given the color blue to these slave drivers: blue, the color of the air, of smoke, of laziness, of nothingness ...

We have seen that anybody who suffers from the Monday morning feeling is soon considered a weakling or a fusspot. In the most advantageous case, you might be able to consider yourself a "victim of the spreadsheet-dictatorship." In Part III I shall take a closer look at the opinions about the Monday morning feeling held by experts, venerable doctors, and learned professors in the sciences of prosperity and success.

7 The first hours at the office

[The coffee machine in the corridor; Blanche enters stage left.]

ROSE	And good morning to you.
BLANCHE	Yeah, good morning.
ROSE	Coffee?
BLANCHE	Please.
ROSE	What is your code?
BLANCHE	243.

[Rose enters code.]

ROSE	Good weekend?
BLANCHE	The usual.
ROSE	Not much …
BLANCHE	Nothing special.

[Rose gives the coffee to Blanche and takes a cup for herself.]

BLANCHE	You?
ROSE	Visited the relatives.
BLANCHE	Your mother?
ROSE	Yeah.
BLANCHE	Still poorly?

ROSE   The usual.

[Rose drinks her coffee.]

BLANCHE   How's your project going?
ROSE   Can't complain. And your department?
BLANCHE   The usual.
ROSE   I'll be getting back to work then.
BLANCHE   Me too.
ROSE   Have a nice day.
BLANCHE   You too.

8 Small's lament

The Monday morning feeling is part and parcel of an arduous life. Let us listen, for a moment, to the lament of an elderly employee about his Monday morning feeling, because it has a specific color:

My name is John Small.
I'm in charge of training for The Company.
My age is 55.
Recently we got an *interimmer* as Director.
We have to make more profit.
And work more cheaply.
And get results.

About my every suggestion
   he asks:
What'll it cost?
What'll it achieve?

To my every question
   he says:
What'll it cost?
What'll it achieve?

With everything I do
    he checks:
What'll it cost?
What'll it achieve?

He uses pretty words,
That's true, when singing about
    Responsibility
    Entrepreneurship
    Agreements
    And Collegiality.

John Small is the name.
My lease car has been taken.
My room has now been cleared.
My work must be *de-intensified*.
But whatever I imagine
    I wonder:
What'll it cost?
What'll it achieve?

This doesn't seem to me a pleasant way to end years of loyal service. There is undoubtedly a lot that you could say about this man: he shouldn't have been so stupid, he should have put up more of a fight, he should have left earlier, and he should have got a different job. But what is true is that he works in a company that is infected with the spreadsheet disease. Something like that causes a *permanent* Monday morning feeling.

Part II
Sad affairs

Oh, it's Monday. I'm going back to bed
then.

And so you suffer from the Monday morning feeling. For some people, it is a tolerably short period of just a few hours; for others, it has become a permanent feeling. What factors are at the bottom of all this? Can we analyze where the Monday morning feeling comes from?

Certainly. We shall investigate who and what are responsible for our disgust, fear, rage, and sorrow. And since it is always much easier to point the finger at others, that is where we will start: first we'll point at colleagues, then at bosses, and finally at companies as a whole.

And if something isn't clear,
feel free to ask Miss Jones

9 Corrupted colleagues

The time has come for us to set down the archetypes of irritating colleagues. Generally, we only talk about this in veiled remarks and sniggering whispers. I prefer to adopt a far more stringent tone. We shall see that a whole range of colleagues can cause us to undergo the Monday morning feeling. The types are listed in the table below. In addition, I have shown in this table the main emotion they induce in other people. Obviously there will be differences. You can decide for yourself which emotions these types generate in you. A characteristic of the Monday morning feeling is, as I wrote in the first chapter, the presence of a certain sorrow, since you always lose something. What exactly that loss is will be dealt with later; we include it, however, in the table.

	Fear	Disgust	Rage	Sorrow
Holier than thou		* * *		* *
Jealous bitch	* * *			* *
Licker	* * *			* *
Skiver			* * *	* *
Macho	* * *			* *
Trend snifter		* * *		* *
Fossil			* * *	* *
Border guard			* * *	* *

Holier than thou

Ethical colleagues swarm around us and our work like flies around rotting meat; flies that have not enjoyed a square meal for years and are now eager to teach us a lesson. They shove themselves forward to participate in projects that deal with the core values of the company. These colleagues are so focused on the "good, the true, the beautiful," that they lose sight of the dark underbelly of our organization; no, they have suppressed it. It shouldn't be there and woe is you if you dare to say anything in their presence about the dark side of people and the company, or even hint at it. Just imagine that your colleagues and bosses were given ideas by this open talk about layers and lies. That would be catastrophic. And so ethical people in the company like to gag, often with barely disguised aggression, anybody who has the slightest doubt about the doctrine of corporate values. They would prefer to expel you from the order—or better, from the company: for this sort of scum, there is no room at the inn.

The holier than thous are so enchanted with the perceived sanctity of their values and so convinced of the moral necessity to implement their project plans and directives without any delay that the necessary ability to nuance their thinking has evaporated, and they are just as unable to consider moral questions as a pride of hungry lions who find themselves in the middle of a herd of tender, juicy antelope.

Fanaticism and ethics are worshipped too intensely, with all the disastrous consequences this implies. Much evil is done in the name of good. Even those supporters of a reasonable and honest company—that is not in itself a bad thing—are more exposed to totalitarian thinking than they might expect. Everybody who talks about a "desired culture," about "mission and happiness in companies" is on a slippery slope. And this is particularly true when they no longer talk for themselves, but on behalf of The Personnel, The Company, The Society: "This survey among the personnel demonstrates that there is a strong need to adhere to the following values." And then the same old values are paraded for all to admire: openness, integrity, team spirit, and customer orientation. The danger with these people is that they lack the moral modesty that is essential for quality within a company. Anybody who wishes to create a company that is not only financially sound but also functions morally, would be better off leaving a lot of things unclear and vague.

So when your stomach turns at the thought of such cynics, then cherish that feeling. It shows that your inner measuring instruments are in perfect working order.

The jealous bitch[3]

If you had to feed all those jealous colleagues, you wouldn't have much left for yourself. Over-zealousness and jealousy are strong emotions, and there is no lack of these on the work floor. I once joined a new company, and one of my new colleagues asked me: "So... what you are going to do here? What is going to be your contribution?" I have never received a warmer welcome. Jealousy is a strong emotion in people and even related to pity! Sometimes such colleagues do a complete about-face and become sincerity and compassion itself. How come? Well, people who are jealous have their eyes focused on your prosperity and fortune, and measure themselves against this and conclude: "I am less happy than you." The sympathetic types do exactly the same, but then in reverse. They focus their attention primarily on your adversity and reach the conclusion that you have a greater portion of tribulation than they. People who are jealous or sympathetic are always thinking about themselves and never about others, except when drawing comparisons.[4]

But it is the jealous bitch that causes us the most problems, for she doesn't just begrudge us our fortunes, she actually reproaches us and suggests that we do not have ourselves to thank for them. "You did well, but then you had more resources, you could choose your own people, you had a godfather or a godmother that protected you when things got difficult," chant our envious colleagues in unison.

For the next year, I'm not in for anybody!

The licker

She nods like the boss nods, she walks like the boss walks, she speaks like the boss speaks: the licker. The colleague who is thinking more about her next job than about her current one. Everything is *in place*, she thinks, as she takes her seat behind her immaculately tidy desk, brings out her golden pen, opening her delicately thin briefcase to remove a calf's leather wallet. The licker looks out of the window and sees her beautiful car shining in the sunlight; OK, it's in the third row, but it's still very near to the Company's main entrance. In three, four years, she will have one of those precious parking spots, where a license plate indicates its rightful occupant. She is correct, precise, and polite. Never an impetuous remark, never an expression of approval or displeasure on her face. Any contact with her is business-like and to the point; never a wasted minute. The licker quickly becomes team leader, coordinator, and program manager. Her only concern is whether she reaches her goals on time and stays within the budget. She will have her way—come good or ill. That is why we should be wary of the licker. A healthy paranoid attitude is never amiss in the organization: it can protect us from unnecessary suffering. In former times, this attitude was known as prudence: caution. It is particularly relevant when dealing with lickers.

Ah, there he is, the life and soul
of the party, off to his nursery

Skiver

You've overcome all shame, washed away the bitterness of Monday morning with countless cups of black coffee, and then you meet the man or woman who has turning being busy doing nothing into an art form. Immediately you suffer a relapse in your recovery from the Monday morning feeling, ambushed by an unreasonable resentment and envy. How is it possible that this pain in the neck is still here and has not been given its marching orders? The skiver is two-faced. On the one hand, he or she is industry itself, pushing around papers, moving files, and pounding like mad on the computer. On the other, he or she is expert in supposed weaknesses: "My back is killing me, my stomach's upset, I've got a splitting headache." It is almost as if these lamenting Jeremiahs take pleasure in their afflictions. They whisper with down-turned eyes to everybody who gives them a chance about how their "great suffering" is real: "Mother is really in a bad way, my wife really wants to leave me. My neighbors really make a lot of noise. I hardly get a wink of sleep anymore."

The skiver is irksome, awkward, and takes away any pleasure others may have in their work—if that pleasure ever existed, which in the current economic climate is seriously open to debate. The skiver would like nothing better than to have us weeping at his or her feet, like some Jesus in a medieval, Christian painting. We may pass a blue judgment on the skiver. Or should we see in this type our example?

Macho

Testosterone cannons may be great in bed, but are a nuisance in the office. They pose and parade and are ready to relate their stories of success to one and all. They tell stories that always follow the same trusted pattern: I went out, I had an adventure, I returned home safely. In his corporate tales, the macho is always the conquering hero, never the lame duck. You will never hear him telling stories in the canteen, in meetings, or at a reception about his failures: "I was given a big project with enormous responsibilities for hundreds of millions. I was put in charge. Everything failed and now they're clamoring for my head." No, they'll never tell stories like that, not there, not then; only when they have gone through the greatest valley of despair that even the strongest macho cannot withstand and have entered the shelter of a shrink's office will they finally crumple and shed buckets of tears about how tragic their career has really been.

Macho man—what are you doing? Are you really a slave to your hormones, to your passions? Do you always have to play the hero? Can't you do without the admiration of your female colleagues and the envy of your male colleagues?

Just imagine that as a female you were lumbered with a man like that! And if it were only his stories, then you could always walk away. But what about those glances that seem to violate your breasts, let alone all those suggestive remarks. Should you say something about it? Again? Ignore it? Complain to the boss? And every Monday morning he is there again: Mr Macho Man.

The trend snifter

Trend snifters are certainly neither original nor creative. They simply have a tiny talent for sniffing out the buzzwords that will be the rage in the coming season. They read the right magazines, meet the trendsetters, and attend seminars that train the leaders in the latest fashions. These colleagues put considerable emphasis on learning to learn and innovation.

Strangely enough, trend snifters often use old-fashioned wisdoms, such as: "there is no road to success; success is the road," or "a river that streams is a river that changes," or "change and renewal are characteristics of our age." The ease with which they talk about the future is, when you hear it for the first time, extremely impressive and you immediately feel that an appeal has been made to you: "Join in, change yourselves, just do it!" But on the second or third hearing you suddenly perceive the pattern: the thirst of these people for this promising future disappears as soon as opinion leaders indicate with their slogans a different road. Then they march behind different flags. It is better to think of such colleagues as somewhat odd, rather than to take them seriously. They are driven by the fear of being left behind and instead of thinking "So what, then I'll just stay on shore," they see a doom-laden image of a bitter and boring present in which, if they do not watch out, they will remained trapped. No, trend snifters are, in the depths of their soul, dissatisfied, frightened nobodies, who always dream of greener grass elsewhere ...

Living fossils

And now a totally different breed: the fossils that surround you. Men and women who are so wedded to old habits that any attempt at change—no matter how small—immediately meets with their resistance. Any proposal you make is instantly dismissed with a "we tried that ten years ago." I once knew a woman who used this remark to derail any idea I put forward. A rather more subtle approach adopted by fossils is a procedural remark about whether "this is appropriate for our company." And the more power such a petrified being has, the greater its ability to fan the Monday morning feeling in you.

These rigid colleagues will use anything at hand to sound the call to their conservatism: the corporate mission, their experience (which for them and for everybody else, is nothing more than systemized prejudice), or legal regulations and restrictions.

I once had the pleasure of having such a fossil as a colleague. It took very little, despite the protestations of happiness and hope that passed his lips, to find yourself dashed against his petrified heart. For if anybody wanted anything different, his face would take on a stony stare and he would address and oppose the person concerned in an injured tone. He thought of himself as someone special. His insights were above any criticism, he felt. He was so convinced of his knowledge, vision, and life experience that he tried to undermine in all possible ways anybody who dared to think differently. He was, no matter how incorrect the metaphor may be, the living example of a fossil. You could also say that his protective instinct was too fully developed.

Sounds like utter nonsense to me,
but fine, we'll take a vote on it

The border guard

At primary school you had those boys or girls who would draw an imaginary line across the table and then snap at you: "this half is mine, and that's yours." Even at that young age, they bubbled with collegiality. They have most probably found a place in some traditional organization, where most of the processes are not much more than a repetition of this original primary school drama. The border guards are those that are very well able to distinguish between thine and mine. They know to the letter what your responsibilities are and what theirs are. And don't you dare have the nerve to trespass on their territory. If you ask them something that doesn't quite fit in with their competence profile, then they will fling back the folder with an explosive and indignant gesture and snarl: "That isn't my task." When the day is just drawing to a close, they will already have tidied their desks, logged out, and packed their bags. They are above average in their promptness and accuracy. With a slight nod of the head, they leave the room.

And if you take over some of their work, because, for example, they are on holiday or off sick, and think you are doing them a pleasure, then you are completely wrong. You are rewarded with an argument. That happened to a friend who, with considerable difficulty, filled in for a colleague and as thanks only received a copy of an email addressed to her boss in which her colleague referred to the fact that she had taken over some of his work during his absence and demanded to know exactly where his authority lay. It resulted in many meetings.

The moral is: never do anything for a border guard. It only causes more discomfort in your work. Just as they cause more of that Monday morning feeling.

Have you heard?
Mr Jones is sick in bed!
Mr Jones is sick in bed!

10 Nauseating bosses

Now we have reached those people in the organization that we like to blame for everything—the bosses. And in a certain sense we are perfectly correct. They're the bosses, not you; they have the power. They are responsible for the way the business units, departments, or whatever name they are called operate. They are responsible for your discomfort.

Unfortunately, and unjustly, bosses are shifting this responsibility away from themselves and think that you as employee should be responsible for everything: your turnover, the way you function, your health, and your career. It is hardly surprising that people ask themselves why we still have bosses.

Let us make a list—just as we did for our colleagues—of the various types, so that we know precisely who puts us in a bad mood on Monday morning. In the following table you will find the most common types. Once again, we indicate which emotion is most present in our Monday morning mix, but with the note that everybody can make a profile for his or her boss with the most suitable mix.

	FEAR	DISGUST	RAGE	SORROW
Moneymaker			* * *	* *
Clammy boss		* * *		* *
Guru junkie		* * *		* *
Bully	* * *			* *
Chair defender			* * *	* *
Crawler	* * *			* *

Moneymaker

A whole herd of bosses now call themselves managers because they believe they serve a higher function than simply leading employees. They are convinced that humankind is here on earth to serve shareholder value so that they can find happiness in the here and now. A moneymaker does not lead but manages and always knows where to find the keys to success: he or she manages the *key* business processes on the output in which the *key* indicators in the performance cockpit take a leading role, so that the Company can remain a *key* player in the *global economy*.

That's the way moneymakers do it. They are the key children of an economy that doesn't deal with anything: not with beautiful products, not with fine services, not with fascinating innovations.[5] The only thing that counts for them is the one-dimensional value of the shares. The moneymakers feel supported by the *opinion leaders* in and around big business. It is shocking when you hear the neo-liberal elite in our country blabbing: "The only way to let the economy grow is to compete on the free market. And success is measured on the stock exchange."

Let's be honest: the current economy is based on greed, on the drive to acquire as much as possible: money, status, and fame. Classic virtues such as frugality and justice have no place in this and are simply for retired entrepreneurs. They are therefore not represented in the character of moneymakers. What's more, companies don't pay them to exhibit those virtues. The high salaries that have caused such continuing (and boring) commotion are part and parcel of this pattern of stimulating

85

covetousness. You ask yourself whether this really must be our fate? Is the liberal market economy the only way?

Of one thing we are sure: that the moneymaker pays no attention at all to work content. Craftsmanship is incidental, just as customers are a necessary evil. The real New Economy without customers has not yet started. And if moneymakers pay any attention at all to their employees, then it is simply to get them to increase production. Every human relationship is, for these "managers," nothing more than an instrument. That's what they have learned from their management gurus. Although they would never admit it out loud.

Ah, the best years of your life, the busiest period in your existence—that is your gift to the Company. But you should consider that when the cow has been milked dry, when the udders swing uselessly under that body, that there would no longer be a place in the stall. And do you hear them bleating, those HRMers, the mental coaches, those moneymakers: "This exit is good for you so that you can develop your talents further. Be thankful that we are getting rid of you." It is hardly strange that these craftspeople get downhearted because a true value is no longer placed on their craft. And that is why we are always so sad on a Monday morning: because we are aware that in addition to the inevitable loss that is always associated with work, we are also losing something more: our craftsmanship.

The clammy boss

You all know them—the bosses who have attended a seminar on happiness or who have spent enormous sums on management professors in the science of prosperity and are now, once again, interested in you, in your deepest core, in your "unfathomable being." Clammy bosses yearn to be a servant leader because they have a calling in life: concerning themselves with your well-being. They are a sort of foot licker, but different. What clammy bosses do is intrude into your most personal private life. You could easily say that in its intrusiveness it is on a par with undesired physical intimacy. Why are they interfering? What on earth have they to do with you as a person, with your ambitions, your desires, and your idiosyncrasies? The boss isn't a padre, vicar, or a shrink.

Every time such a clammy boss comes to you with more drivel, then you get this weak feeling in your stomach that, with small shocks in your midriff and esophagus, tries to find an exit. This is a reasonable reaction from your body: if something unpleasant comes too close to your body or even forces its way in, then your body wants to get rid of it. You experience this passion, as I mentioned earlier, as distaste and disgust. Cherish this suffering, no matter how unpleasant: it is a faithful ally to circumspection.

Miss Franklin, we're all
extremely happy with you

Guru junkie

You can take it from me that most bosses are as insecure as the youngest operator, and know in the depths of their souls, even though they would never admit aloud, that they are just muddling on. This is an insight that does them proud. Uncertainty is perfectly reasonable and the opposite, the certainty of knowing what has to be done, is just as bizarre because it is so irrational. Bosses who precisely understand the market, the company, and their people suffer from arrogance and inflated egos. The world is simply unpredictable and is held together by coincidences. Who knew back in 1990 that Internet hype was imminent? And who could have told us then that it was all a South Sea bubble? Who is prepared to predict with any certainty whether next year's economy will flourish or fail?

It is because of this uncertainty that many bosses seek comfort and refuge from mental coaches and other "prosperity experts" who are excellent at one thing: insinuating that they can reveal a path that leads out of the desert of being a boss. They are wholesalers in management concepts, step plans, two-by-two matrices, color codes, audits, and tests.

One year, the herd rushes after those travel guides who shout: "Culture—do something about the culture in your company." The next year, they bleat: "Competence management: assessments for everybody." And then chant soothing words about ethics and sing psalms with the local choir about integrity and compliance. The newest graduates of the "prosperity faculty" preach norms and values. And if that isn't enough, then there are those unsavory types who have to climb up on a soapbox and, like some prophet of doom, reveal the dark side of humanity and persuade everybody to become a rat. Or they sound the alarm about some sort of supposed malaise.

And so bosses eagerly gather at conferences held by gurus and their disciples, in the hope that they will offer a glimmer of certainty. These guru junkies in turn terrorize their organizations with their new-fangled methods, new-fangled techniques, new-fangled tests, new-fangled forms, and new-fangled jargon. Time and again. And their subordinates simply shrug their shoulders and think, in unison: just piss off. And they're right.

Bullies

With some bosses, it is hard to imagine, as you see them parading around, shouting commands, issuing orders, that they were once tiny, pink, new-born babies. I recently met a particularly exquisite example of the species when I was allowed to address the management team of a retail company about people orientation in their company and she, the CEO, was going to attend. I had looked earlier at the company's website, just to see whether the company had a people-oriented look about it. No way: just texts about and photographs of equipment, business processes, and money. The page about contacting the company won the prize: you saw a vague photograph of a reception desk, and if you looked closely, you saw that there was nobody behind it! That showed just how people-oriented the company was. And when I discussed this in some detail, the managers tried to suppress their giggles, but their Tsarina grew redder and redder: "How dare you. That is absolutely not true. Have you gone mad? Show me the proof, go on, show me, I want you to show me the proof," and with that she pulled her laptop out of her bag and hurriedly surfed to the corporate website. Weeks later, her managers told me that once I had left, she had exploded, demanding to know why they had just sat there grinning and why they hadn't made sure there were more people in the photographs on the website. Wonderful, a superb example of the bully.

A characteristic of bullies is that they are always convinced they are right, that things will always go better if done their way, and that the employees are really incapable of doing even the simplest tasks. Bullies mainly induce irritation and rage in their employees because they are unjust, stand in the way, and treat

You just have to shout back at him

them with contempt. They rob everybody of their honor because they show nobody any respect. Anybody who serves under a tyrant goes to work every Monday morning in a rage: powerless, but full of the most violent fantasies.

Defender of the chair

Anybody in a company who wishes to survive as boss will frequently need to call on his or her defensive and offensive talents. Sometimes you are amazed that people, who are considered incompetent and lazy by almost everybody in company, somehow manage to stay at their jobs for years on end. "What do they have that I don't have," you ask yourself. Simple: they are strategists, survivors, and you are not. I once met a young woman who had been a manager for just a couple of years. "No," she answered when I asked her whether she enjoyed her boss's support:

> I only see him once a year with the figures, and nothing else. He is always off on a trip somewhere, handles special PR projects, and moves in the highest circles. But what he does? Nothing that's of any help to us. He rarely meets a client. And yet he knows how to defend his chair. He is always in the right place at the right time when decisions have to be reached. And he knows exactly who to put on display in his trophy cabinet.

In one way or another, I have respect for these long-term survivors, for the way in which they always manage to find shelter when they need it and to rush into the storm when that suits them better. But as subordinate, you'd be better off without a boss like that. This type of boss is much too concerned about his or her own chair. Defenders of the chair cause irritation.

Crawlers

At first glance, this is rather a strange beast: a boss that crawls.
Our stereotypical images conjure up a totally different idea! On
closer inspection, the crawling boss is revealed as a normal
boss, but then a little different. You will recognize crawling
bosses from their reticent, rather bowed way of moving, as if
they wish to avoid notice. They never walk along the center of
the corridor, but always look for the cover of the walls. Crawly
bosses will come up to you with a smile and then whisper
exactly what you should do—and more precisely, exactly what
you shouldn't do. They will never do this in a meeting, but
always in a place of brief encounters: on the street, in a hallway,
near to the entrance to the canteen. The crawler always plays
off at least two cushions. But you should make no mistake: they
always have their plans ready and have their aims sharply in
their mind's eye.

They know how to manipulate you, because they can create a
feeling of pervasive fear. They readily tell you how well you are
performing and at the same time remind you, in their subordinate clauses, that there is a lot changing in the company. And if
you then feel just a slight pang of fear, then that is nothing
unusual. It is exactly their intention. You must always be a little
scared of what might happen to you. Crawlers control their
subordinates by keeping them in a constant state of threat—it
is called "gallows management."

A woman once told me the following story: "Well, I had a meeting with my boss. We talked about all sorts of things. And then,
she said that I shouldn't spend too much time with a certain
colleague. There were movements afoot to loosen the ties

between the company and him." Her commentary on this was clear and simple: "I knew exactly what I thought when I heard that. If she is now whispering in my ear in order to isolate my colleague, perhaps she'll soon whisper into other people's ears that they should avoid me." Anybody who wishes to encourage a paranoid organization should carefully follow the above strategy. It is hardly surprising that the subordinates of indirect bosses suffer a considerable degree of discomfort.

Honesty forces us to admit that crawlers are not only found among managers but also among professionals, even those who make writing their business. One of the best examples of this was the illustrious humanist Erasmus: people have remarked that he had an exceptionally indirect manner of taking revenge against all sorts of developments that he perceived in his time. There are other, less significant talents, cowards, who suffer from the same disease; it is not proper for me to name them here.

This gallery of colleagues and bosses has not placed the most attractive examples on exhibition. That was never the intention. Our colleagues can irritate us; our bosses can incense us. What we have tried to do here is create a clear picture of the Monday morning feeling. Who are the wreaths on our coffin?

It is now time to consider whether we work at a lamentable company and if so what it is like.

11 Lamentable companies

I don't think I am too far off the mark when I say that in many organizations, something strange is happening. Some companies and governmental institutions pretend that they are a collegial and warm community, others seem to have entrapped themselves in a permanent process of change, and in others, nothing happens very much at all and every initiative becomes bogged down in a quagmire of bureaucratic procedures. And quite a few organizations have transformed themselves into a form of intensive human farm because we are so obsessed with our competitive position.[6]

In the company I worked at before,
we always had a community hug

Community

You are certainly unfortunate if you find yourself in a company that considers itself one big, happy family and wants to be team-oriented and human. The employees and, even more so, the consultants who work here talk a lot about giving meaning and commitment. You have to participate in social meetings, and you are constantly caught up team building or hit with feedback or some other clammy idea.

And if you've been really unfortunate, you may even be expected to do voluntary work for a couple of days each year. The people in HR will go on about why it's so good: it allows the company to "give something back," because it extracts energy from Gaia and must return it, because the Company wants to be social-minded and sustainable. And so you find yourself on your Sunday off trimming hedges in the garden of some old people's home, wrapped in a body-warmer emblazoned with the Company logo, or you find yourself jogging with a few handicapped people through the local zoo. And the healthy thought that fills your mind—that you are an unbelievable idiot for saying yes—is simply too painful for your own personal pride and self-awareness: you have once again allowed yourself to be carried away by the community feeling in the Company. Once again, you have fallen for the implicit claim that the Company will decide what is noble. Why have we, as employees, become such wimps? This thought is so painful that it prevents you from thinking clearly and frugally.

By the way, do you have a PDP—a Personal Development Plan? You know, one of those forms that allow you to fill in your own future, where you came from, who you are, and what your mission in life is. I would feel totally ashamed if I had to fill in one of those. You've already taken so many important decisions in your life—got married, bought a house, started a family, chosen a course of study—and you've done it all without a PDP, and now the Company expects you to fill in something because HR thinks that it will give you a better insight into your existence within the Company. And it gets worse. There are even trade unions who have put down in collective work agreements that every employee has a right to a PDP. A worse example of infantile treatment of professionals has never been shown.

In this sort of clammy organization, there is one obscure rule: you must be human. Just doing a good job is insufficient. There is, however, a "but" attached: you must be human, *but* not one with crazy or cantankerous characteristics. If you show any of these, then you are punished with a course in personal development, or you have to fill in core competencies or recognize that you are a type 2 or 3 in the Enneagram. You should not have the illusion that in this sort of company you can actually be human, certainly not if you want to define this in your own terms. Communities like to hold a monopoly on the power to determine who is human and who is not.

The best thing to do is simply shrug your shoulders and if it all becomes too much go into mental banishment. I rather like the thought of taking mental leave: gazing out of the window, drinking a lot of coffee, daydreaming.

So if you work for a human company, it's best on Monday morning, even though you are feeling harried and bad-tempered, to put on your human face and become the ideal employee that you hate so much. Adapting is a matter of professionalism.

Permanent reorganizations

There is a joke that circulates among consultants: which reorganization are you working on now? There is a very large grain of truth in this. You too are working—or have worked—for a company that is facing the umpteenth makeover. It is remarkable that the top layer, with a few very favorable exceptions, remains unaffected. During recent years, many layers of managers and employees have been fed through the grinder of assessments. Bosses and employees who have worked for years in their company, have had to spend a day or so taking tests, proving their talent for acting in role play, and giving socially correct answers in interviews with success experts from a psychological assessment agency. It has been decided in advance that a quarter or a third will have to drop out. It is a power technique to fire people through the back door and to instill the fear of God into those that remain.

I still consider these assessment circuses a strange affair. You would think that leaders would be fully aware of the qualities they have at their disposal. Anybody who works with people will know within a year or so their habits and peculiarities, what they can do and what they can't do. You really don't need to hire a psychological assessment agency to tell you that. The only explanation I can give is that leaders are on the one hand filled with a deep fear of rejecting loyal employees, and on the other a burning feeling of guilt for the perceived betrayal. Hiring in an external agency that uses so-called scientific tests to do the dirty work brings welcome relief to a tortured mind.

But if only these money-wasting rituals were the end of it. Unfortunately, that is not the case. When you're caught up in

Sometimes just a rumor about a
forthcoming reorganization does the trick

the umpteenth reorganization, you are confronted with yet another list of nonsensical directives and standards. You have to fill in even more forms and from next Wednesday, you may only use form 345 version 2b when making your budget proposals. And special change newspapers, websites, and meetings chaired by babbling television personalities try to thrust the same old new jargon down your throat: result-oriented, competence management, integrity, downsizing. You listen wearily and think of just one thing: if only it were Friday.

A lot of people have become weary of change. If only all those changes actually made a difference. A lot of transitions have simply failed: mergers have been undone, old bureaucratic rules have been taken out of the cupboard; employees are once again set production targets.

Consultancies know all about those failures: try searching Google on the words "change process" + "failure" and you won't believe what you see. What is so interesting is that whenever most consultants write about failed transformation, they generally propose an alternative change scenario. "You have to concentrate more on the aims," writes one. "No, no, you have to attack things in stages," insists another. "No, you have to involve the employees in everything," babbles a third. And they all miss the point: we are sick of change.

Bureaucracy

Bureaucracy has long suffered a bad press. It is far too slow and rigid, too concerned with itself rather than with results. This is all true, but this is not the reason for the greatest complaint. No, the sorrow of bureaucracy lies elsewhere. To understand this, we first have to go back to the essence of bureaucracy: it is an ethical machine.[7] Ethical? yes, because bureaucracy ensures that every method, decision, and result is predictable and transparent. Every personal influence by the employees is filtered out. You wouldn't really like it if the tax inspector, when assessing your tax returns, put you into a different tax band simply because he couldn't stand you. There is no place in bureaucracy for such affinities, caprices, and arbitrariness. The employee must follow precisely the procedures laid down for him or her in the regulations, otherwise a serious dressing-down will follow or, worse, disciplinary measures. Bureaucracies are rational organizations in which everything is precisely prescribed and in which employees have carefully defined functions or roles.

The consequence is that, once you enter a bureaucracy, you lose an important part of your humanity. It is not the intention that you take your peculiarities and your moods to the floor where you office is located. Once you enter a bureaucracy, you are transformed from a person into a functionary. Everything you love in yourself, your moods, your superstitions, your sympathies and antipathies, are of no value whatsoever.

Certainly, bureaucracy is a very ethical invention and we should not dismiss it out of hand with accusations that it is rigid and slow (you could ask yourself, would you rather that it were arbitrary and fast?). But we must realize that this invention comes at a great price, since it dehumanizes everybody who works in it. Whoever works in a bureaucracy is put into a pigeonhole of use and responsibility: every cog turns for the greater good, every cog can be traced, and every cog can be called to account.

There are attempts to make bureaucracies more human, more like a community. But believe me, if this humanity were to result in an erosion of the bureaucratic regulations for clarity and honesty, then this humanization will soon be at an end: that's not what we want!

And so hundreds of thousands of men and women pass through revolving doors into their offices: swallowing hard, because they once again feel the sorrow of the bureaucracy.

Intensive human farm

In our economy, a new type of company has emerged that is related to neither the bureaucracy nor the community—the intensive human farm. The bureaucracy is about something—about achieving results in an honest and transparent way—and even the community is about something—producing beautiful things at a profit in a human way, taking the many into account. However, the intensive human farm is about one thing and one thing only: producing money. Customers don't count, citizens are nothing more than citizens, we do not acknowledge governments, and employees are resources that we milk dry. The moneymaker mentioned earlier feels completely at home in this biotope that is riddled with the spreadsheet disease.

Anybody who works in such a company is expected to set everything on one side for the good of the Company. That means, they say, that you must above all else be flexible. Evening hours, weekend hours, all hours are at the disposal of the moneymaking machines. I know a director who considers it perfectly normal that when he gets up on Sunday morning at seven o'clock, he gets his two children out of bed and, while they are playing at his feet, logs in via wifi and studies the mail and comments on various documents. A further characteristic of the intensive human farm is that everybody and everything is under permanent surveillance: every intervention, every result, every mid-term result is quantified and reported. Middle managers have, in this human farm, largely disappeared and have been replaced by spreadsheets. Let us be honest: many companies are nothing more than milking stations that attach their pipes to our creative and human nipples and drain away the milk.

Part III

Ludicrous therapies

Wake up your dad – he's got to get to
work

We have seen how we suffer from the Monday morning feeling, what it means, and how it develops and progresses. It has also become clear that the feeling is a symptom of a much more pervasive feeling of malaise in work. We have pointed the finger at bosses, colleagues, and corporate cultures. It is now time to take a closer look at the remedies against the Monday morning feeling and work malaise. We will get a better insight into the incredible hair-brained schemes that are currently being taught in business school. Anybody who thinks that the magic has gone out of high-tech organizations should think again. Let us giggle at and work ourselves up about the following matters:

- Just do it!
- The company is a living organism.[8]
- Happiness in spiritual matters.
- Return of the bureaucracy.

In the last two parts of the book, we can then delve deeper into our passions and find some comfort for the inevitable malaise.

We shall drink ourselves paralytic on Freud.

You're not a bad leader. But you've got
to learn to look a little bit happier.

12 Just do it!

It is remarkable that most authors of management books ventilate in a naive way all sorts of scatterbrain ideas for creating reality.[9] If you were to ask these writers to give their opinion on the Monday morning feeling, they would try to convince you that you do too little, that you have inadequate skills to ensure that work and private life go hand-in-hand. They will always say that you are to blame, because you don't make use of the proper methods. But if you were to use their method as described in their recently published book, then ...

The whole world is fairly level-headed about our abilities to influence human events, except, that is, managers and management thinkers who live in self-imposed mental quarantine. There the magical superstition that managers can influence their employees, customers, citizens, even governments, in their favor has still not disappeared. Quite the opposite in fact; the ink of one prosperity manual has hardly dried before the next appears in a puff of smoke. In their attics and garages throughout the land, prospective gurus are now practicing their latest creation spirals, Jacob's ladders, and quadrant knots, dreaming all the while of the great stages of new management thinking where they will soon appear as "the star." "You know," said one bookseller to me, "it doesn't surprise me that the wheel is constantly being reinvented, just that each new wheel is still being put to use." That hits the nail on the head. Much of the management cacophony is nothing more than a repetition of things trumpeted elsewhere and people long to hear the same old trumpet call time and time again. That is why the "school of prosperity sciences" will always have pupils and why they will always read the same books.

The song these pragmatic doers sing is always the same. What you must do above all else is formulate clear and concrete goals. Often, you are provided with a list of criteria against which good aims can be judged (specific, measurable, realistic). Next you must clearly define your current position and develop a stage-by-stage plan. For each stage, you describe the steps you will take and any gurus worth their salt will always cover themselves by saying that is not easy to take these steps and that you must be aware of adversity and misfortune. But if you mobilize sufficient support in your surroundings, then you will get through it all. Remember to celebrate your successes. But especially when you remain on track. These, in a nutshell, are the recommendations of people who believe that you should just do it and that your success depends on your own efforts. You must, of course, carefully follow their self-help books.

And yet we must put the finger on the sore spot. We all know by now that these instruction manuals simply don't work. But why is that? Let's take a few pot shots.

First, these doers suggest that our actions show a high level of predictability. Often they are very implicit about that, and not without reason. Because if they were to state their hidden assumptions explicitly then they would soon be revealed as idiocy: do these activities and you will prosper. The big problem is that this predictability is hardly present—if at all—in the real world. I dare to predict that this will never happen. There are all sorts of coincidental influences, people simply don't get along with each other, you accidentally hear something, you are unlucky with your roommate who turns out to be a lout, you start you career at the height of an economic boom. You thought that he or she would persevere, but he or she throws in the towel sooner than expected. No—organizations are far more messily constructed than we like to admit. We should reinstate Lady Luck, spinning her wheel of fortune.

Then there is another point—and I will slightly lift the veil about the inevitability of our malaise—that we cannot keep our passions under control. They have their own timetable and considerations that are closed to rational inspection. All at once we are angry, then we are bored or over-zealous, or rather clammy and too enthusiastic which makes us do things that are not in the interest of the company or of ourselves. We try, with more self-control and appointments, to make things more predictable, but we shall never completely succeed. Don't be deceived: procedures, measuring systems, contracts, and integrity campaigns are for no other purpose than controlling and excluding the unexpected in organizations.

We must conclude that the step-plans of the pragmatic teachers offer us little solace. We make ourselves feel guiltier, because we believe that we are the cause of our own discomfort.

13 The company is a living organism

A lot of people have written and lectured about the dehumanization of our work and the importance of the human touch. We work harder and feel better when a company is also a society in which the employee is also treated as a human being. The occasional hug will do wonders. A company is not just a business construction of people who, under contract, interact with each other to achieve results. It is also a web of human relationships with all that entails: sympathies, antipathies, excitement about results, and sadness about losses. Employees who are expected to make use of their potentials and ensure that these are up-to-date are happier, more satisfied, and therefore more lucrative for the company. If you were to ask them how they viewed the Monday morning feeling, they would say that it is all because your company isn't human enough and your inability to develop your abilities has given rise to all this resistance. A good company, they would say, is a form of living organism. There are many companies who like to project that they are not really a company but rather a circle of friends.

The recommendations in the humanization programs are broad and vary from the use of warm words, pats on the shoulders,

Difficult day, Monday?

through intensive culture sessions to personality programs that delve very deeply, to the design of the office. You all work together in one large open space with lots of plants, beautiful designer lamps, and gallons of cappuccino. You regularly have dinners together in the evening with your colleagues, and you do the sort of things friends do: play cards, go bowling, or cook together. Or, during the winter, you go off to the Alps together for a long weekend of snowboarding and serious drinking. And there you sit, all together, in some deserted hotel, working on team building. The neglected maintenance of individual relationships is carefully undertaken, accompanied by sighs and groans, painful silences, and many tears. "I'm getting angry again, John, because you copped out again and I had to do everything." Trainer: "It really hurts, doesn't it? You're getting really angry, aren't you?" In this way, employees are constantly being reminded that they are not just professionals, but more importantly human beings.

Let's quickly take aim at these humanity adepts so that we can dispatch their ideas to the mass grave of idiotic notions.

First and foremost: work is nothing more than work. We don't need to be human in absolutely everything. We would be exceptionally surprised if the plumber burst into tears as he started mending our tap and, when we remarked that it isn't really as bad as all that, that he should launch into a long story about how his wife etc., etc.

Second, we draw all sorts of conclusions about our personal being. With all those personality trainings and coaching we quite wrongly turn it into something fascinating: something that should scare us (there are all sorts of frustrations, defense

How long have you been working for us
. . . eh . . . what's your name again?

mechanisms, and vulnerable undercurrents that prevent us functioning properly) and at the same time that conceals some hidden treasure (our character has its authentic and pure components). This results in a specific expectation that can only lead to disappointment, namely the expectation that our personality is something that we can program and manipulate ourselves. Quite the contrary: by the time we reach adulthood, the harm has already been done and there is very little for us to adjust and reconstruct.

Third, humanization is more likely to increase rather than decrease our discomfort with work. That is because, as we have said, our companies and organizations are modeled on the drive to acquire as much as possible. Whether you work for a company or serve the government, everything is about results. And all attempts to humanize things will eventually be subject to this demand for performance. We do not need to have any illusions about this: humanity lasts as long as the wallet remains filled.

Humanism in companies is suffocating and causes more discomfort through disappointment as a result of impossible expectations than comfort from kept promises. It fans the Monday morning feeling rather than extinguishing it.

14 Spirituality

For quite some time, corporate prophets have been claiming that if we were to design our organizations in a more spiritual way then we would have greater satisfaction in our work since we would then be connected to the "It" and to the "Being." This fairy tale is more popular than ever, and I regularly meet those behind it: the inspirational preachers. Men and women who wish to stimulate our spirituality.

I once met a fine example in a bar on a rainy afternoon. He sat next to me and stirred his coffee. "I used to be a hippy, then went into IT and made piles of money. But that's when it all started. I simply didn't know what to do." It was clear that this man was suffering the fate of the wealthy. Nothing ever happens to them. One might start a gallery in Whitechapel, the other will study art history, and yet another may set up a foundation for the performing arts. In this way, these people can create the impression that the rich really matter.

"So what did you decide to do?" I asked him.

"I sold my house and moved to L.A. to get a taste of excitement. I stayed there for four years. Then it was over. Dabbled a bit in charity. Not for me. Now I want to bring people in companies into contact with their soul, their essence. My passion is spirituality. I want to do something with it. Perhaps hold a workshop or something like that."

Could spirituality cause our Monday morning feeling to disappear? Could we perhaps achieve a permanent endorphin state? We would have to give up thinking, of course, because that only deforms reality with its divisions and delusions. We must open ourselves to the "undivided being:" meditation techniques, smoking incense, and exercises in the art of experiential perception. And we must, above all, risk the journey inwards: that is where the gold of our divinity can be found. Only when we have recognized and acknowledged this can we be a good leader to our employees and a good supplier to our customers.

Spirituality is a fairy tale in which even professors in our area believe—something they had better not do if they really want to maintain any dignity for their title.

First of all, spiritual managers assume a dual reality: the reality of the workfloor and the reality of heaven. That other, that more beautiful reality can only be understood once you stop thinking: "letting go," is the name given to this, as if our thinking is constantly held in a cramped grip.

That's very good, that is: we have to accept that something exists even though we mustn't even think about it, let alone research whether it actually exists or not. I've got another one for you: Father Christmas really does exist, but you first have to give up all your critical faculties, otherwise he doesn't exist! Anybody who follows the road of spirituality betrays the human condition.

Ah, there's our Mr Brown.
He's going to inspire us.

Second, there is something strange is this spiritual thing. It suggests that the world is a warm, comforting, human place. Whose idea is that? It's just as probable that, outside our everyday reality, there is nothing but blind mechanisms, aimlessness, and emptiness. A wilderness where only survival, cruel lust, and destruction matter. It is beyond rational knowledge, a place where everybody can come face to face with anything, both good and evil. "The horror, the horror," was what the evil Kurtz called it in Joseph Conrad's *Heart of Darkness*.

Third, the spiritual path is in itself violent. This remark may surprise you. But the idea is anything but stupid. "The more possibilities we have, the higher we rise above ourselves. Even our insanity is too moderate. Break down the dividing walls in the mind, cause the mind to tremble, yearn for its destruction— the source of all renewal! At the moment, our mind is turned against the invisible and it only perceives what it chooses to perceive. If it is to open itself to true knowledge, then it must be split asunder, pushed beyond its limits, and suffer orgies of destruction."[10]

If we want to deal with our discomfort in the organization, we must simply ignore these childish—although far from innocent —lessons of the spiritual thinkers. Their starting-point is far too unhealthy to provide any sort of foundation. And if you confront the spiritual types with their nonsense, then they frequently answer that they do not really mean it like that, but that they really want a more human company. "Well say that then," is my immediate thought. "It you really want us to treat each other like human beings then you really don't need all this spiritual kitsch."

15 The return of bureaucracy

Now I have arrived at a new direction that has only appeared relatively recently. The Monday morning feeling—this discomfort we feel—could very well be due to the fact that we have too quickly discarded bureaucracy. There is one way of getting through our working life, and that is by applying once again the basic rules of bureaucracy. This is the solution offered by Judith Mair in her book *Het is mooi geweest* (*It was fine*) (2003).[11]

The recipe offered by the new bureaucrats is very simple. We have to restore bureaucracy to its place of honor, first of all by clearly separating our working lives from our private lives. At work, we work and do our duty. At other times, we live and are a complete human being. We work from nine to five, and overtime is exceptional. We act civilly to each other and are always polite and formal. "Good morning, sir." "Good night, Ma'am." And we do not concern ourselves with the emotional lives of our colleagues, employees, and managers. We prefer to wear formal attire, which we refer to as our "business clothing." Every Monday morning, we ease ourselves into our straitjacket, put on our mask, and carefully hide away deep within ourselves that which we hold most dear.

You must be new here

The reintroduction of the bureaucratic model is a choice between two evils: either we accept that life is essentially unpleasant because everything starts to feel like work or we protect our personality and our private lives, our freedom, by once again resolutely and demonstrably lowering the barriers between work and private life; and thus we only suffer the malaise during office hours. "No, I shan't be attending the social meeting; I do have a private life, you know," is your answer the next time the company wants you to put in an appearance after work.

And yet, and yet—once again this is a path that we would do better to avoid. The least significant reason is that it is simply no basis for it. Employees have been so entrapped and ensnared in the doctrines of humanity that they blindly rush after the development of both themselves and their lives—cheered on by the doers along the line: Just do it! Just do it!

A more serious objection is that the new bureaucrats do not take account of the mixture of life styles in their analyses. Let's be honest: work and private life overlap each other. This is caused both by the nature of work and modern technology. Most people are more involved with processing data than with hard physical labor. The latter is generally clearly connected to a specific location; information work is not: with a GSM, a laptop, and a wifi-hotspot, you can work almost anywhere. These developments will mean that work and private life become even more interwoven rather than less. No—I do not believe in the panacea of Judith Mair, that everything would be so much better if there were a strict division between work and private life, simply because it just won't happen.

And finally we should be skeptical about the possibility of people shrugging off their personality at the office entrance and that their personality will then play no role in the department. It would imply a psyche that is made up of at least two separate units—one for home, one for the office. A psyche that allows the owner at will to turn on one or other of the parts. No, if we follow the new bureaucrats—no matter how correct their analysis may be—then we will find ourselves in a cul de sac.

So—what is the solution?

Part IV

Impulse ergonomics

Eddy, it's Monday. I have to get to work.

It is remarkable how rarely biology is present in our thinking about organization and management, even though it could offer some revelations about organizations in general and our Monday morning feeling in particular. A pleasant exception is the book *Driven* by Lawrence and Nohria (2002),[12] which offers insights into our elementary, biological, drives and how these play out in organizations.

I have often asked myself why evolutionary biologists seldom give lessons in business schools to future leaders and professionals. After all, if we, as laypeople, wish to understand anything about human behavior, then we should learn something from them.

I ascribe this absence to a wicked fear among management thinkers of processes and events in organizations that cannot be influenced, and to this belongs, unquestionably, the passions of the flesh. It is also in their own interests: managers and professionals do not like to hear that things can happen over which they have no influence. That is not why they attend exorbitantly priced seminars. Imagine how the audience would react if they were told: "There is nothing we can do about it. You will just have to learn to accept it. It is simply part of your nature." Trainers, mental coaches, and gurus are painfully aware of this.

Driven is, as we have said, an exception because it takes evolutionary psychological principles as its starting-point.

The authors distinguish four elementary drives:

- the drive to acquire
- the drive to commit

133

- the drive to learn
- the drive to defend.

The explanation for the existence of these four drives is quite simple: in evolution, the people who happened to be equipped with the most appropriate drives survived and were able to breed. Apparently, these four drives were very desirable. We have inherited them—unconsciously, aimlessly, and without any predetermined plan—from our successful forefathers. During a lecture, the director of one of Holland's largest zoos grinned at me and said: "Do you realize that behind us there are hundreds of thousands of ancestors with all their favorable characteristics who are still working in us. Ten thousand years of civilization with agriculture and cities have not removed those things from us." In other words, even in our high-tech and rational society, the same drives work in us today as when our ancestors were crossing the savannas.

16 Four drives

Let us quickly turn a spotlight on those drives that still well up in us.

Acquisition drive

The drive to acquire something is deeply rooted in our being. Whether it is about food, drink, resources, sexual partners—there is always a basic drive that drives us on. Perhaps you may say that there is no drive working in you when you try to acquire something because you always consider things very rationally. I have to disappoint you: you won't get very far without drives and emotions. You need those drives to bring anything to fruition. People with brain damage that causes a malfunction of drives and emotions, simply cannot reach a decision, even though they have carefully weighed all the alternatives.

And if Mr Johnson puts his hands on you,
you have to say something about it.
He knows very well he shouldn't do it.

Commitment drive

If the acquisition drive is all about survival and self-interest, then the drive to commit is the direct opposite. We know from our own experience that we achieve better results when we collaborate with others than when we work alone. Somewhere inside us, there is a drive to form communities and groups. The explanation is simple: anybody who gave way to these drives had a greater chance of surviving in a hostile environment than somebody who did not. Even now, most people are incapable of living a lonely life and people who isolate themselves for too long get strange ideas. This is clearly illustrated by the story of Antonius, the hermit, who lived alone in the middle of the Egyptian desert and who had all kinds of strange ideas and visions.

Somewhere inside us, this drive always finds a voice that tells us that taking on a commitment will ultimately benefit us more than it will cost us. The famous philosopher Spinoza (1632–1677) expresses this perfectly in one of his propositions about ethics: "Only when people live under the guidance of reason will they constantly and necessarily adapt to each other."[13] He probably means nothing more than that the drive to commit is a reasonable drive, since it drives us to adapt to each other so that we can ultimately achieve more together.

Survival drive

The third drive that is active in us is that of survival. We all know it. When somebody approaches or enters our territory we experience a feeling of aggression that forces us to protect all that we own. We could, of course, give this some impressive label, either before or after, but that is simply a rationalization of an older and instinctive feeling. In organizations, we still experience this territorial drive, whether when merging two departments that cannot stand each other, or when two employees precisely define their tasks and responsibilities and keep a careful watch on each other: in either case, the cat is among the pigeons.

The strange thing is, we cannot get by without enemies. Who would we be if we had no people, groups, or companies as our enemies? Then we would be unable to distinguish between mine and thine, between ours and theirs. And if we do not have any enemies, then we invent them. That happens in world politics—but also in local affairs. The potential for defense has to be mobilized from time to time, whether it is useful or not.

Transformation drive

Our basic drives should include the drive to learn and change. The underlying reason is that organizations that are capable of being investigative, that can separate the wheat from the chaff and are also capable of storing this knowledge either internally or externally, are better off. It seems to me that this drive is closely linked with "inquisitiveness," or may even be its emotional equivalent. We are inquisitive when we observe things with raised eyebrows and a certain reticence and only then approach them with care. People who are capable of learning have a better chance of survival, certainly when they find themselves in different and new situations. This drive does not become less when we grow out of childhood. It is constantly present throughout our working lives.

17 Organizational drive ergonomics

Our Monday morning feeling is nothing more than an indication that we cannot put our drives to good use in our company. We want to do something and we can't. Or exactly the opposite: we don't want to do anything but we must. This is enough to make you bad-tempered! We can identify a tragic mismatch between our flesh and the organization. Isn't the sigh "I don't feel like it today" nothing more than a vocal expression of something we have felt in our bodies, a partial surrender to our drive, to our desire to do something else? Anybody who suffers from the Monday morning feeling can in any case conclude that his or her drives are in perfect working order. The trouble is, you can't do anything about it.

How does this mismatch work with each of the four drives?

We can now offer a drive-driven explanation for our discomfort in work. Many people suffer at work because "they have to play second fiddle," or their ideas "never go anywhere," or "simply disappear into the bottom drawer." They get depressed because their acquisition drive never finds any satisfaction in anything they do. You want to make something worthwhile or

I've got a suggestion, Mr Jones.
Why don't we knock off early today?

useful, you put in a lot of time and energy, you give the best of yourself only to discover that it's all come to nothing. That happens to you once, even twice, but then you think: "Forget it. Do it yourself." A lot of people go to work feeling like this and swallow deeply every single morning. The spreadsheet disease of the modern economy is unnatural.

Sometimes companies ignore the drive to commit. You know them well, those companies that seem to have as much cohesion as grains of sand. You enter an office and walk through empty corridors; all the doors are shut. Everybody is sitting isolated like a monk in a cell. When people become isolated in this way, they will complain about being alone, about how boring things are, and how they feel alienated. This also provides an explanation of why the humanization programs of all those gooey managers don't work. These propose a degree of commitment that requires too much commitment. Or they simply can't deliver on their promises.

Very many companies that have proudly proclaimed themselves a reliable, caring, and human company have, during the last few years of recession, been forced to fire many employees. They have drastically changed their management style: they have become business-oriented. On the workfloor many of those who have remained behind ask themselves: "How is this possible? We used to be a warm company where anything went. Now you can't do anything. He's gone, and so has she. It's been demolished. I gave everything I had to this company." In such companies, there is an overruling feeling of treachery. And it is not without reason that in the world of management a lot of thought is being given to how on earth you can *reconnect* your

No, he's out to lunch

employees. I hope that the answer they come up with is: with considerable reticence.

Employees who are devoured too much by their company, who find too little stimulation, or are misled, are at great risk of being repulsed by their work.

And another reason for the malaise at work is revealed. Many people do not become weary from the content of their work, as long as it is their choice, but from the game of attack and defense that has become part and parcel of it. If you talk to people aged 55 and above, then the first thing they will say about their job is: "when will I be able to stop?" And if you press them on it, then you will never hear that the work is so hard but that everything connected to it is: the daily fights, the fisticuffs with the border guards, the nagging committees, the alliances between the crawlers and the bullies that you constantly have to sidestep and disarm. Much of the work done by professionals revolves around attack and defense. Often, too great a demand is placed on the drive to survive.

And do people take into account the capacities of people to learn and change? We assume that the drive to learn and transform is limitless. That is certainly what you see at those transformation consultancies that drive employees round the bend. We have a drive to learn and change, but there are limits. We have the ability to run—but nobody expects us to run at 50 mph. Why then, is our learning ability put to the test in such an unpleasant manner?

The reverse is equally true. Who has never thought—or thinks now—that the work they do is simply a repetition of the same

Elly, is it nearly five o'clock?

moves? You've had it with your company and want something else. It is as if your drive to learn and transform has nowhere to go.

Adapting to drives

The remedy for more pleasure in our work is a corollary to all this. We should organize work in such a way that it matches our natural drives. You could say we should try to operate a form of organizational ergonomics. After all, we adjust the height of our chair and buy shoes of the proper size. Why do we not take into account our drives? We would be much more satisfied and far happier in our work.

Drive ergonomics is nothing new and is applied naturally to a certain extent and within certain limits in our organizations. Employees can do as they see fit, as long as they achieve results. That last point is also the most important limit: whichever way you look at it, you will eventually have to take responsibility for not achieving results. Nevertheless, the authors of *Driven* suggest that our organizations could be much better attuned to our four elementary drives.

How would that happen? Would we let the strivers battle it out for power? Would we put the commitment-and-bonding types in the HR department? Would we give the inquisitive ones jobs in the research department? Would we send in our machos to handle negotiations? In fact, you simply apply the golden rule of a good HR policy: the right person in the right place. If you manage that, then everybody will be able to put his or her drives to a satisfying use and everything will start coming up roses.

Is the solution—apart from implementation considerations—really so simple, so elegant, and only a question of dropping everybody in the right place?

No, it's not.

A major objection is the implicit supposition that drives and needs can be satisfied, so that they are silenced thus allowing us to wallow in extreme pleasure. If only that were so. But hasn't the much-publicized drive exhibited by many top executives to grab everything possible demonstrated that when greed is satisfied it is not extinguished but actually encouraged? Freud was wrong when he said that frustration about satisfying a drive actually resulted in it increasing. If there is one place where we should be able to witness Freud's theory of moderation, then it is among the top dogs. Yet they have discredited the theory in practice: bonus whets the appetite for more bonuses, power for more power, fame for more fame. When drives are satisfied, they become even stronger.

A second objection is that the large gap between the flesh and the organization cannot be bridged with any ergonomic measure. The reason for this is found in Chapter 18, which deals with the inevitability of malaise.

Part V

Between flesh and organization

Back to work on Monday.
Will you manage that?

The major problem with our drives is the mismatch with our modern organizations. A whole range of laws, behavioral codes, and applied procedures are aimed at channeling our drives and keeping them under control. You could say that there is a major mismatch between our organizations and us.

It would, moreover, be incorrect to assume that this mismatch between our drives and organizations is a modern phenomenon. As early as the sixth century B.C., a gap was identified between man and culture. The Greek philosopher Antiphon said: "Many matters that are good according to the laws are hostile to our nature."[14] What he meant was that we lay down all sorts of laws about what we should hear and see, what we should do and shouldn't do, and that such laws are necessary for human interaction, but that frequently they do not match our nature. And anybody who strolls through what people have thought and written about what makes us humans tick, will soon discover that quite a lot of attention has been given to the mismatch between the nature of humankind and the way they have arranged their relationships with other people.

Nice work? We don't do that here.

18 Malaise in the organization

Well, to get to my point. The Monday morning feeling, this general malaise in companies, is nothing more than the inevitable companion to professionalism.

People who act professionally have distanced themselves from their primary drives, and are caught up in a constant process to keep their greed and aggression under control. In this way, managers and professionals try to turn themselves into competent, functional, and focused people. That this is no easy matter is shown by the frequently fruitless yet endless training that managers and professionals put themselves through in order to control their direct impulses. Let me put it this way: professionalism and malaise are like Siamese twins that cannot be separated even by the most advanced surgery. The price we pay for our targeted and instrumental behavior is the Monday morning feeling. We are two-time losers: we lose our drives, and then we lose the illusion that we can control and rule our drives.

Much more useful

I am not optimistic about the ancient mismatch between our drives, our passions, and our organizations, our civilization. In 1947, the German Roman Catholic theologian, Josef Pieper, wrote an essay about leisure and culture. In the hesitant rebuilding of a decimated Germany, he saw with remarkable clarity that many areas were becoming more proletarian. He meant that the work ethos was becoming increasingly central to society, so that everybody and everything was subordinated to rational planning and utilitarianism. His question was whether there was more than just work. He wrote:

> Is there still something within reach of human work, yes, of human existence as such, that is not legitimized because it is inherent in the targeted mechanics of a five-year plan? Is there something like that, or not?

The concern that he expressed with a far-sighted view more than five decades ago still holds true today: "Would it be possible to save mankind from becoming nothing more than a worker, than a function?"

I think it remarkable that somebody in a period of destruction and guilt, such as that in postwar Germany, should have noticed the gradual domination of the utilitarian perspective. You would have thought he had other things to worry about. And yet Pieper noticed things that we now meet in all areas of life. If you want to be any sort of organization, then being result-oriented and efficient is not enough. The majority of organizational improvements, such as the introduction of balanced scorecards, reversals, process orientation, have no other expectation than to make as many aspects of the business as possible both predictable and controllable in meeting the goals that have been set.

But our private lives have also been unable to avoid such methods of usefulness and efficiency. Many parents plan their daily activities in a way that would not be amiss for the most seasoned project managers. Every activity is programmed with the aim of "getting as much out of life as possible," as one young professional woman once told me. Life mustn't be frittered away, but should create as much happiness as possible, and should thus be run like a company.

And so we chase our illusions of usefulness, achievability, and predictability—illusions that justify the reasons for controlling and managing our drives. Drives, those old, stubborn layers in our nature, are of no use in the glass office palaces on our industrial estates.

Anyone who works loses. Anyone who loses suffers. Anyone who suffers seeks consolation.

19 Acceptance and consolation

What are we going to do about that Monday morning feeling that always pursues us and never lets us down? We'll have to learn to live with it. Whenever something happens to us that is unavoidable and unpleasant, then we must find a way of coating the bitter pill, of calming the beating breast, of allaying the fear, of tempering the disgust, and softening the sorrow.

Anybody who wants to do something about the Monday morning feeling will first have to accept it and then seek consolation. And fortunately we can mine a long and important tradition.

Oh, I'm not really in the mood today

Accept inevitability

The most important thing if you suffer from the Monday morning feeling is to have a clear understanding of the reason why you don't feel like doing anything: your passions want to take you in a direction that doesn't match the duty of Monday morning. Of course you don't feel like it, of course you don't want to be surrounded by all those nasty colleagues, not to mention the managers and bosses. The worst you can do is to feel guilty about your own desires. Then you will have a double burden to bear: the burden of unsatisfied desires and the burden of feeling guilty about them. We really do not need to shoulder any unnecessary loads.

Accept rigidity

An old trick for handling your emotions—and thus a way to deal with the Monday morning feeling—is to think hard about the root of the emotion and about possibilities for changing your fate. If this proves impossible—and this is generally the case—then the emotion has little use.[15] The Monday morning feeling arises out of a mismatch between our drives and the demands made by our offices, factories, and governmental bodies. Since this mismatch cannot be changed, then the emotions arising from this are senseless. There is no point in being depressed, angry, fearful, or filled with disgust. Anybody who realizes this will find some relief and may be able to endure this mismatch more easily.

It could always be worse

A very old trick for dealing with malaise and adversity is to compare your Monday morning feeling and the discomfort you have in your work with larger disasters. Or to quote the words of Seneca (an old, somber man): "Look around you, and I say this with emphasis, at everything; you will find no household so pathetic that it cannot find comfort in the greater adversity of another."[16] Look at the fallen angels who used to rule giant corporations and now sit at home twiddling their thumbs because of a tragic reversal of fortunes in their careers. Cheer yourself up by thinking of all those bankruptcies and evictions, the cancers, and any broken bones you can find. Nothing offers such relief as the greater suffering of others.

Diversion

Another way of brightening up your Monday morning is to ensure sufficient diversion so that you can, for a while, forget your despair. Most people have, by now, become quite expert at this. Some people start the day by telling in detail everything that happened at the weekend so that that pleasant period is extended—at least in the imagination. Others start doing little jobs that didn't really need to be done: designing a new structure for email folders or watering the plants that are already half drowned. And yet others think it's so quiet in the department that they can merrily surf websites showing things that would never, ever take place in an office, at least not during working hours.

Create distance and retreat

The best way of escaping the mismatch between drives and organizations is to ensure that you are in the office as little as possible. Rich people understand this very well: if you want to enjoy yourself, make sure you don't have to do any work. I know one entrepreneur who thinks that everybody should continue working far into old age; but he has arranged his own exit to take place long before he reaches 65. You see—that's real wisdom. And young people, too, understand exactly how the world operates. They postpone as long as possible the moment when they will have to start working. "Before you know it, you'll be caught up in everything. You'll have kids. And then you're trapped for years," said a friend who had just finished studying business sciences.

If it is impossible to escape work, then it is important to create a spiritual and emotional distance from it. You will survive the mismatch best by pretending that you give everything to the company while you know very well that the truth is rather different. Many people who, in the coming years—thanks to a worsening economy—are forced to work longer and longer hours, will find solace in this approach.

I knew I'd find you here.
Why aren't you in the office?

Sublimate

A rather refined way of coping with unpleasant situations is by sublimating your drives. This is nothing more than directing those of your drives that are frustrated into a direction other than that originally intended. If you are frustrated in your desire to enter into a collegial relationship with one of your team members, then you must direct your desire at something else: a plant, for example, or a tree in the atrium. This is what people do when they start tree hugging: they sublimate their unrequited passions. Other people turn to spirituality, and search, as we mentioned earlier, for their prey in humanity and on the planet Gaia. And if you become aggressive and want to punch somebody's head in, then use this destructive energy to implement all sorts of changes: nothing is as awesome as change and renewal.

Anyway, if you have too many frustrated passions, then perhaps you should consult Freud who developed the whole idea of sublimation.

The art of idling and woolgathering

I have just mentioned the critical analysis that Pieper made of the utilitarian ethos. He also came up with a remedy that could help assuage the Monday morning feeling. We should take more rest. And by that he didn't simply mean time off and leisure because this is only intended to get employees ready for more work. No, the rest he suggested was an interruption in all the daily target-oriented tasks that arise when we contemplate the timeless, the hidden, the mystery. For Pieper, rest is the antithesis of the ideal employee who is active, result-oriented, and dynamic within a carefully prescribed role. In contrast to work there is "rest as the expression of the non-active, the inner calm, the relaxation, the 'let it happen' and the remain silent."[17]

It is a pity that Pieper expressed all this in a mystical fairy tale, but you could perhaps expect that from such a religious man. But he does set us on an interesting path, one that is far more materialistic and therefore far more realistic. We should escape more often from the rationality of organizations; not by adopting some New Age mumbo jumbo, but by spending more time idling and woolgathering. We should mess around more, just let things happen. Daydreaming in bed, fantasizing about all the great schemes Pieper could have brought to fruition: this is where the idler finds comfort for all those missed chances. We must take the art of doing nothing to a new level.

Virtual expression of passions

If all the previous tonics are still not enough to ease your troubled soul, then you could always become just a normal employee—one of those people who have forgotten that you are a creation of your own hormones. Normal employees work hard and correctly. Their desk is always neat and tidy, they work through their tasks according to their relevance and urgency, and their social skills are exemplary. In other words, they are the ideal son/daughter-in-law, the ideal neighbor, and the ideal employee all rolled into one.

But when they get home, something gnaws at them, as if their shoes are too small or their jacket is too tight under the armpits or the elastic in their underwear is cutting into the white flesh of their stomachs. Then they creep to their PC and surf to their 19 inch full-color universe of unbridled passions and lusts, accompanied by Dolby 5.1 surround sound audio. Finally they have escaped from the humdrum world of work and become free. In this way, ideal employees achieve that moment when their passions are once again under control and they seem as innocent as a newborn baby. Tomorrow—yes, tomorrow is another day.

Tomorrow is Monday morning. Every day is Monday morning. Once again we feel the tension take hold of us. It is as if the Devil is whispering in our ear, as if he is writing us letters from Hell. He commands us to do exactly what is not required of us. And that is why we always feel sorrowful and uncomfortable: civilization means, quite simply, saying farewell to our passions and learning to live with an inevitable mismatch. That is the price we pay for the way we live and work. Now more than ever before.

Gott sei Dank geht alles schnell vorüber
Auch die Liebe und der Kummer sogar.
Wo sind die Tränen von gestern abend?
Wo ist der Schnee vom vergangenen Jahr?

Bertholt Brecht, *Nana's Lied*

EPILOGUE

"Come through, and we'll fetch her." I follow the orderly to the hospital's mortuary. Today's the day and I will see with my own eyes things that most others only know from pictures: the inside of a human being.

"If you'd like to put on this apron, this cap, and these slippers, you can go in."

The final instructions about hygiene are given. It can start. I will be helping a younger colleague make an analysis.

"We first make an incision in the upper part of the chest, on both sides."

The old woman lies naked on the dissecting table, a white towel over her face. The pathologist stands there like Dr. Nicholas Tulp: serene and powerful.

"And then we open her chest cavity because we want to take a tissue sample from her lungs. This woman died yesterday from cancer. But we want to know the exact cause of death. The family has, of course, given its permission."

My colleague and I look at each other; are we still alive or have we fainted? She nods reassuringly at me and I pull a face. The chest opens with a creak. We look inside: a deep fleshy cavity filled with red liquid and little chunks. The autopsy assistant siphons away some fluid. I am immediately reminded of homemade minestrone soup. My friends and colleagues were wrong. Everything seems quite familiar to me: the heart, the intestines, the lungs, and particularly the interior of the chest, with its ribs and red meat. I know where I have seen this before: in the supermarket. Spareribs, that's what they are. Spareribs.

"Then we neatly fill up the cavity with cotton wool and swabs so that everything seems perfectly normal. We sew up the incisions and pass the lady over to the undertaker."

And that's what happens. The deceased is rolled out of the autopsy theater and, once we have washed and changed, we follow her. She's been given back a face. The undertaken is busily applying some make-up.

I decide to wander around for a while and walk through the corridor into a brightly lit hall. The sun is shining directly through the windows, projecting neat squares onto the floor. Around me, three silent bodies lie on stainless steel tables. The old man on the left is still wearing his slippers: just arrived. It is deathly quiet. Specks of dust dance in the beams of sunlight. I turn round and feel myself becoming heavy. With a crash, that ancient question, the question of all questions, has landed in my mind: what is humankind? I take a deep breath and walk with a heavy step back to the room where the undertaker has now finished his work.

I look into the coffin: what is humankind? And then I know the answer. Humankind is flesh, nothing but flesh.

Joep Schrijvers, Amsterdam

NOTES

1   *Johan Henser; text/music*: K. Krijnen/W.v.d. Biggelaar, P. Coenen; trans. J. Ellis.

2   Boëthuis: *The Comfort of Philosophy*—a classic in the comfort category.

3   First published in *Intermediair*, August 2004.

4   I would suggest to everyone that they consult *Tusculan Disputations* by Cicero—a classic text about emotions.

5   For one of the many criticisms of the shareholder economy, you could refer to Weggeman's book *Provocative Consultancy*, chapter 5. (M. Weggeman, *Provocatief adviseren, organisaties mooier maken*, Schiedam: Scriptum, 2003.)

6   With thanks to Jaap Peters who coined the term "intensive human farm."

7   Paul du Gay, *In Praise of Bureaucracy*, London: Sage, 2001.

8   With thanks to Corinne Maier (*Bonjour paresse: de l'art et de la nécessité d'en faire le moins possible en entreprise*, Paris: Editions Michalon, 2004).

9   A fine example is the book *Just Do It!* by Ben Tiggelaar (*Doen! Nieuwe, praktische inzichten voor verandering en*

groei, Utrecht: Spectrum, 2003)—available in an English translation by Jonathan Ellis.

10 E. Cioran, *Bestaan als verleiding,* Historische Uitgeverij, 2001.

11. Judith Mair, *Het is mooi geweest: het kantoor is geen pret-park,* Schiedam: Scriptum, 2003.

12 P. Lawrence and N. Nohria, *Driven: How human nature shapes our choices,* San Francisco: Jossey-Bass, 2002.

13 Spinoza, *Ethics,* proposition 35, part 4.

14 Antiphon, *Fragments B.66,* in *The Older Sophist,* ed. R. Kent Sprague, Indianapolis/Cambridge: Hackett.

15 In the stoic tradition of comfort, the meaningfulness of emotions is central. If these do not make any contribution (and that is generally the case), then they are not worth having. And when you are aware of this, your emotions calm down and your mind comes to rest.

16 Seneca, *Annaei Senecae de Consolatione ad Marciam,* XII-4.

17. J. Pieper, "Rust en cultus," in *Rust en beschaving,* trans. T. Slootweg, Soesterberg: Uitgeverij Aspekt, 2003, p. 41.

ABOUT THE AUTHOR

Joep Schrijvers has written numerous articles about personal development, coaching and learning. He has worked as a researcher, trainer, video director, manager and consultant, and now lectures and writes about corporate politics, irrational behavior and the role of chance in change processes. He has a special interest in corporate narratives, many of which have found their way into this book.

INTERNATIONAL BESTSELLER

"Consider what the runaway hit *The Rules*, a shameless guide to getting hitched, did for romance. *The Way of the Rat* promises to do the same for the world of work."

The Times, UK

"I strongly recommend this book for its novel style and words of wisdom . . . It is not only extremely perceptive of human behaviour at work, but it is also fun to read."

Management Today book review by Professor Cary Cooper, organizational psychologist

"Schrijver's book speaks frankly, and with an admirable lack of motivational nonsense, about the real dynamics of business success."

Daily Telegraph, UK

THE WAY OF THE RAT
A SURVIVAL GUIDE TO OFFICE POLITICS
Joep P.M. Schrijvers

Tired of reading about the habits of highly effective managers? Given up trying to accomplish anything in one minute? Don't care who moved your cheese? Here's the antidote to management books. Learn the real way to make friends, influence people and achieve your career goals: *The Way of the Rat*.

With caustic wit, black humour and uncanny insight, the author takes you down into the sewer to explore the dark and devious rituals of business today. He shines a light into corners of the office that most companies would prefer to ignore – places where jealousy, cruelty, anger, hate and revenge lurk. How can you subvert your boss? Exploit your colleagues' weaknesses? Come out on top? It's easier than you think. Be ruthless; be a rat.

Don't be fooled by talk of empowerment, teamwork or corporate values. Office politics isn't like that. It's about power: how you get it and how you use it. *The Way of the Rat* tackles the subject with refreshing honesty, and no small dose of cynicism. Read it – but don't leave it lying on your desk.

ISBN 0-9542829-2-2 • £7.99 PAPERBACK